When I'm Feeling
ANGRY

Written & Illustrated by Trace Moroney

FIVE
MILE

When I'm feeling angry
I feel like there is a
boiling hot volcano in my tummy
that is about to . . .

explo

When I'm feeling angry
I want to kick and scream and

stomp . . .   **stomp . . .**

stomp my feet so hard
that the whole world shakes.

I want to run and run, and never stop.

Everyone gets angry sometimes.

Some things just make me
so mad . . .
like when
someone
makes fun
of me . . .

or when someone ruins my sandcastle . . .

or when I get blamed for something I didn't do.

Feeling angry isn't wrong.

But letting my anger hurt someone else is.

When I'm feeling angry
I try to remember to do the things
that make me feel better . . .

like taking great big breaths . . .
in . . . and . . . out

or
going
to
my
favourite
quiet
place.

Talking about **why** I'm feeling angry,
with someone who cares about me,
can help make some of
the anger go away.

And, sometimes, I get **soooo** angry that I forget what it was that made me angry in the first place . . .

and **that** makes me laugh!

Can you tell what the Bunny is *feeling* by looking at each face? Match the words to the faces:

NERVOUS   **SCARED**   **SAD**

HAPPY   **CALM**   **ANGRY**

Here are some questions you might like to ask your friends or family . . . or even yourself!

★ What are the things that make you feel angry?

★ What are some things you can do to help calm yourself?

★ When you feel really angry, what can make it worse? And, what can make it better?

★ Describe a time when you felt your angriest? What do you wish you could change about this? If you had to deal with this same thing again – would you behave or respond the same way? Or in a different way? How would you do this?

★ Remember: It's okay to feel angry, as long as your anger doesn't hurt others . . . or yourself.

BACKGROUND NOTES FOR PARENTS

EMOTIONAL SECURITY IS THE KEY

One of the greatest gifts you can give your child is a felt sense of emotional security. Children who feel delighted in as they explore their worlds, and cared for in their painful feelings, become emotionally secure. You can help your child feel secure by supporting their exploration through play, imagination, and learning. You can also help your child feel secure by being available in times of need, when painful feelings overwhelm, and they reach out for comfort and care.

Helping your child gain the self-confidence needed to deal with failure, loss, shame, difficulty and defeat is as important - if not more so - than feeling good or being the best. When children trust themselves to handle painful feelings - fear, anger and sadness - they gain an inner security that allows them to embrace the world in which they live.

Each of these *Feelings* books has been carefully designed to help children better understand their feelings, and in doing so, gain greater autonomy (freedom) over their lives. Talking about feelings teaches children that it is normal to feel sad, or angry, or scared at times. With greater tolerance of painful feelings, children become free to enjoy their world, to feel secure in their relationships, and to be happy.

Professor Craig Olsson, PhD.
Professor in Developmental Psychology, Melbourne, Australia

FEELING ANGRY

Healthy self-esteem reduces defensiveness and anger. Anger is one of the most difficult emotions to come to terms with. Children need to know that everyone gets angry sometimes, and that it's a natural feeling. By giving children the chance to put their side of the story, they not only *feel* valued but get to vent their anger in a healthy way. By helping children find their own solution, and then to act on it, they build the *self-trust* needed to have angry feelings but not to be controlled by them.

Bill Hallam, Child Psychologist & Professor Craig Olsson, Melbourne, Australia